AF621696

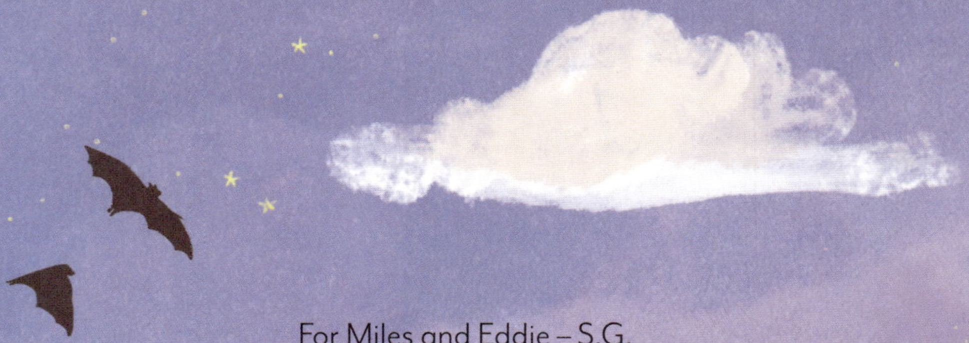

For Miles and Eddie – S.G.
To Tom and Sammy, love C.R.

First published in Great Britain 2026 by Red Shed, part of Farshore
An imprint of HarperCollins*Publishers*
1 London Bridge Street, London SE1 9GF
www.farshore.co.uk

HarperCollins*Publishers*
Macken House, 39/40 Mayor Street Upper,
Dublin 1, D01 C9W8, Ireland

Red Shed is a registered trademark of HarperCollins*Publishers* Ltd.

Text © Saskia Gwinn 2026
Illustrations © Carolina Rabei 2026
Consultancy by Dr Nick Crumpton and Philippa Forrester.

ISBN 978 0 00 876746 4
Printed and bound in Malaysia.
1

A CIP catalogue record for this title is available from the British Library.

All rights reserved. No part of this publication may be reproduced, stored in a retrieval system, or transmitted, in any form or by any means, electronic, mechanical, photocopying, recording or otherwise, without the prior permission of the publisher and copyright owner.

Without limiting the exclusive rights of any author, contributor or the publisher of this publication, any unauthorised use of this publication to train generative artificial intelligence (AI) technologies is expressly prohibited. HarperCollins also exercise their rights under Article 4(3) of the Digital Single Market Directive 2019/790 and expressly reserve this publication from the text and data mining exception.

Stay safe online. Any website addresses listed in this book are correct at the time of going to print. However, Farshore is not responsible for content hosted by third parties. Please be aware that online content can be subject to change and websites can contain content that is unsuitable for children. We advise that all children are supervised when using the internet.

FSC www.fsc.org MIX Paper | Supporting responsible forestry FSC® C007207

Into the Dark

SASKIA GWINN & CAROLINA RABEI

RED SHED

CONTENTS

NIGHTTIME BEGINS

The sun is setting, the sky is dimming and animals are heading back to their homes for a cosy night's sleep . . . but some creatures are only just waking up. For them, there's a busy night ahead!

You might be going to bed, but so many of Earth's other wonderful creatures are getting ready for a world of animal adventure; hopping, pouncing, singing, playing, feasting, buzzing and travelling through the night. These animals are **nocturnal**, meaning they sleep during the day and are most active through the night.

Are you ready to step into the dark to discover an action-packed world of animal adventure?

THE MOON AND THE STARS

You may have noticed it's not *totally* DARK. That's because the Moon reflects the sun's rays and shines down on us with its brilliant bright light. Even on a cloudy evening, this acts as a night light . . .

BARAU'S PETRELS

These amazing birds migrate long distances separately, only to all arrive at their destination at the same time when the Moon is full (see page 18).

SANDHOPPERS

These crustaceans have a Moon **compass** in their **antennae**. They spend the day buried under the sand, then come out at night, using the Moon to help guide them as they forage for food, such as seaweed, in dim light.

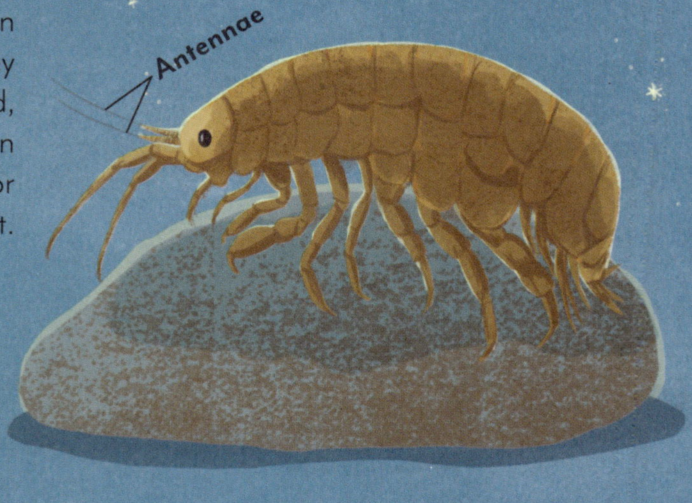

Some clever animals use the stars to see where they are going . . .

BIRDS

Birds use stars to navigate by remembering their positions in the sky, so they know which way is north and which way is south.

BOGONG MOTHS

When the stars are hiding, it's thought that creatures such as these moths can use **Earth's magnetic field** to navigate their way, just like a compass uses Earth's magnetic field to always point north.

DUNG BEETLES

Some species of dung beetles use the light of the stars to keep them on the right path! Their impressive eyesight means they can see dim stars even on cloudy nights. African dung beetles use the twinkly **Milky Way** as a kind of giant night light so they can roll poo in a straight line back to their burrows, sometimes racing each other as they go!

But which *other* animals are soaring through the night sky while you're busy snoring in your bed?

BIRDS

At dusk, when the Moon is rising and the sun is setting, brilliant birds take off into the sky on their nighttime adventures. Owls start their evening hunts – as their **prey** find it harder to spot them swooping down when it's dark. Petrels travel thousands of kilometres across seas and oceans, looking to land on an island far, far away, and all sorts of other birds look for snacks in nighttime waters.

Are you ready to meet these remarkable birds that thrive in the dark?

OWLS

There are over 250 species of owl in the world – from the teeny tiny elf owl to Blakiston's fish owl, which has a wingspan as long as a gigantic gorilla! Most owls are nocturnal (largely active at night). To help owls hunt in the shadows, they have super hearing.

For most of them, one ear is slightly larger and higher than the other. This helps an owl to pinpoint exactly where its meal is – the ear that is higher captures sound from above, whereas the ear that is lower captures sound from below. Each ear fires off a signal to the brain and then . . . SWOOP! Breakfast is served.

BARN OWLS

A barn owl's heart-shaped face directs sound towards its inner ears so it can hear even better, which is useful in dim light!

GREAT HORNED OWLS

The great horned owl is named after the tufts on its head, which help it camouflage itself in trees and recognise other great horned owls.

OWL EYES

You can usually tell if an owl is nocturnal by the colour of its eyes. An eye has an iris (the coloured part) and a pupil (the black part). If an owl's iris is very dark, it's usually a nighttime (nocturnal) owl, because dark irises mean its prey won't see its eyes shining in the dark. If the iris is yellow, it's usually a daytime (**diurnal**) owl. And if it has an orange iris, it's probably crepuscular, which means it's most active at dusk (when the sun is setting) or at dawn (when the sun is rising).

EURASIAN EAGLE OWLS

Eagle owls hunt at night but are mostly active at dusk and dawn; the irises of their eyes are a pumpkin-orange.

ELF OWLS

Despite being the world's smallest owl species, the elf owl hunts scorpions, mice and lizards, as well as insects.

TAWNY OWLS

Like many owls, the soft-edged wing feathers of a tawny owl help it fly silently.

NIGHTJARS

Nightjars begin their search for food as the sun is setting so they can gobble up night-flying insects such as moths and beetles. This intriguing bird has large eyes compared to its body size, which helps it see in the dark, but it still relies on the light of the moon, especially when it comes to its chicks.

Some species of nightjars time their eggs to hatch when the Moon is at its fullest – the better light helps them find food and ensures their babies are well fed.

KĀKĀPŌS

This flightless parrot lives in forests in New Zealand. It forages in the dark to avoid daytime **predators**, searching the ground for leaves, buds, bark, fruit, seeds and flowers. Though it can't fly, a kākāpō can take long leaps from tree to tree and can climb. If it does spot a predator, a kākāpō has a trick up its sleeve . . . it will freeze, making it difficult to be seen. This was successful for many kākāpōs – they are thought to live up to a whopping 90 years old.

However, many years ago, humans introduced predators to where kākāpōs live and they are now **endangered**. Conservationists have worked hard to save the kākāpō, and its numbers are slowly increasing.

WAVED ALBATROSSES

If you look out to sea from the Galápagos Islands when the Moon is full, you may spot a waved albatross searching for squid. Squid usually come closer to the ocean surface at night, giving the waved albatross an opportunity to grab a tasty meal.

Albatrosses can sleep while flying by locking their wings as they soar through the skies during the day or night. Amazing!

LESSER FLAMINGOS

These birds get their pinky-orange feathers thanks to their diet: red and orange **pigments** in **algae**, and crustaceans that have become pink from eating the same algae. These pigments are also found in veggies such as carrots and tomatoes. Don't worry, these veggies won't turn *you* pink!

Flamingos' favourite time to forage is at night, when they dip their heads into calm, still waters – the flatter the water, the easier it is for them to filter out delicious algae to eat.

BARAU'S PETRELS

When the land is dark, but the Moon is bright, one of the best things to see is the meeting of the Barau's petrel seabirds. Each year, these tropical birds that live in different locations such as Australia and Indonesia, travel thousands of kilometres across the Indian Ocean to arrive at Réunion Island (east of Madagascar) around late afternoon before the night when the Moon is at its fullest.

The Barau's petrel is an endangered species.

Once they've arrived, the breeding season can begin. This is the time when animals of the same species find a mate so they can have babies. Scientists think that arriving at the same time makes it easier for the petrels to pair up.

NORTH ISLAND BROWN KIWIS

It's time for cute-looking brown kiwis to come out of their cosy burrows. Kiwis start the night by tip-tapping on the ground with their very long beaks to find food. Unlike many other birds, kiwis can't see well at night, so they rely on their super sense of smell to find food, rustling through **leaf litter** on the forest floor to sniff out tasty bugs and worms. These birds are omnivores (which means they eat meat and plant matter), so they look for fruit, seeds and berries too.

All species of kiwi live in New Zealand.

Kiwis might be named after the male kiwi's call, which sounds like their name, 'Kee-wee! Kee-wee!'. These birds can't fly but they can run super-fast – at speeds around 20 kilometres per hour. That's more than twice as fast as the average human can run!

MAMMALS

All over the world, many magnificent **mammals** sleep during the day to emerge at night when they hunt, forage, feast and play. From cool, tree-hugging koalas and awesome-eyed leopards to sticky-tongued pangolins and playful foxes, many mammals are well-equipped to hang out in the dark! For some, this is thanks to their specially adapted eyes that can see in dim light or to bodies that allow them to stay awake for hours on end.

Let's discover some amazing mammals that wake up as the sun sets and find out how they spend their 'days' in the dark.

BIG CATS AT NIGHT

LEOPARDS

What's that big cat doing creeping through the shadowy trees? When the sun goes down, leopards look for tasty meals – other mammals who share their forest home, such as monkeys, make a delicious dinner. Leopards have to keep quiet though – one crack of a tree branch will wake up a sleeping monkey who will then alert the whole tribe! Leopards also like to eat fish, reptiles, birds, insects, mongooses and porcupines (if they can get past their spiky quills!).

A leopard's pupil opens more widely at night. This helps this master hunter's eyes to take in more light and reveal their prey.

At the back of the eyeball is the retina. It contains two types of cells: rods and cones. Rods help to see the shapes of things and cones help to see colours. Unlike cones, rods process light even when it's dim during the night. Nocturnal animals, such as big cats, have more rods than most daytime animals, giving them better night vision. Leopards can see seven times better in the dark than humans!

LIONS

If you spot a lion around your lunchtime, it's probably having a nap . . . because a lion's lunchtime is during the night! Like leopards, lions have better eyesight in the dark than during daylight, so although lions do hunt during the day, they do most of their hunting at night. And they eat a lot! One lion meal can make up a quarter of its own body weight.

TIGERS

Tigers will travel for many kilometres in the dark to find other mammals to eat, such as buffalo and deer. Each tiger has a totally unique set of stripes that blend into the high grass to hide them.

GREAT BULLDOG BATS

To hunt in the dark, bats use a clever skill called echolocation to hunt prey such as moths, mayflies and beetles. This means they send out an ultrasonic noise (a sound that is too high-pitched for humans to hear). This noise then bounces off their prey and back to the bat. This allows bats to pinpoint where their prey is, so they can swoop down and gobble it up.

PANGOLINS

Pangolins scurry out of their burrows to reach inside ants' nests with their sticky tongues, which are longer than their bodies! Using special muscles, they are careful to close their ears and nostrils so no ants can crawl into them! Some species, like the black-bellied pangolin, use their armoured tail to help them climb trees and hang upside down from the branches!

AYE-AYES

A special reflective layer at the back of an aye-ayes big, round eyes help it to see better at night. Once an aye-aye is awake, it taps on trees among the rainforests of Madagascar using its super-long middle finger to see if they are hollow. If they *are*, then there could be tasty insects hiding inside – a perfect midnight meal. The aye-aye just needs to remove the bark, scoop up the bugs and gobble them up. Its long fingers can also be used to scoop out the insides of tasty fruit.

WHITE-TAILED DEER

Some animals, such as the white-tailed deer, like to move around at twilight, just before the sun rises or sets – especially in the summer to avoid the heat of the day. They emerge from their hiding places of tall grass and dense woodlands to graze on twigs, fruit, nuts and plants in the safety of the dim light, when it's harder for predators to spot them.

KOALAS

Cute koalas sleep a lot thanks to their diet. The eucalyptus leaves they eat are toxic to most animals, but thanks to an organ called a caecum that is extra long in a koala, they are able to digest them. However, this takes up vital energy! Plus, there are very little nutrients in these leaves, which means koalas need to conserve their energy by getting plenty of rest.

Koalas largely snooze during the day, nestled in branches and hugging trees to keep safe. And when it's dark . . .

When the weather is hot, koalas can often be spotted hugging trees because the tree trunks are cooler than the air around them.

. . . they sleep some more. For 18 hours or more! Eventually, koalas *do* wake up at night – to munch on leaves for hours on end, call out to their friends (or shout to keep other koalas away) and move around. Koalas have weak eyesight, so they rely on a keen sense of smell to figure out where they're going in the dark.

RACCOONS

In the wild, these stripy-tailed nocturnal mammals like to live near water in forests, where they can munch on eggs, frogs, bugs and berries. Raccoons like to dip their food into water before eating it. Some scientists think they're washing it before eating it, but raccoons *actually* do this to find out more about the food. Raccoons have super sensors in their paws, and water increases the quality of these senses. This means that by dousing their food in water, raccoons can find out more information, for example if something toxic has hitched a ride on their fruit or nut.

Crab-eating raccoons live in the jungles of central and south America. At night, they snack on crabs and other tasty treats, like oysters and turtle eggs, that are all found in the nearby marshes.

Forests aren't a raccoon's only habitat. They will eat almost anything, so it's common to find them raiding city rubbish cans at night – crashing around looking for leftover food! Sneaky raccoons are clever enough to open lids, doors and windows to search for food or shelter. They live anywhere from holes in trees to attics in people's houses!

AFRICAN ELEPHANTS

When the sun sets and the stars come out over the African savannah, elephants stay awake – even though they've been awake all day! Elephants are thought to sleep for only two hours a night and spend the rest of their time doing much the same as they do during daylight hours – eating, playing, travelling and finding waterholes.

The African savannah elephant is the world's largest land mammal. The sea-dwelling blue whale is the largest mammal of all.

Sometimes, when elephants travel long distances, they don't sleep for several nights in a row.

Because elephants can sleep standing up, it's difficult to tell if they're awake in the dark or not, so scientists fit special sleep monitors to some elephants to track how long they sleep for. Two hours' sleep might not seem like much, but elephants eat for up to 18 hours through the day and night, giving them the fuel they need to stay up for so long!

PORCUPINES

When night falls, prickly porcupines leave their dens in rocks, trees and hollow logs to find food and to defend their territory! A porcupine's eyesight isn't great, so it uses its brilliant sense of smell to find food such as fruit, leaves, plants and bark.

If a hungry **predator** pounces, porcupines protect themselves with their quills, which can get stuck in an enemy's skin. Porcupines stomp their feet too when they're particularly cross!

SLOTH BEARS

These tree-loving mammals usually wake up at night to nibble on fruit, such as figs and mangoes, and insects. Sometimes they also eat honey (and bees!) by using their long tongues to reach inside the nest.

When their food is digested, sloth bears do what you do too – they poo out the unwanted waste. Because their poo is full of fruit seeds, new fruit plants will grow where they poo!

So, sloth bears are nature's night gardeners!

FOXES

If you hear a shriek in the night . . . it might be a fox. Foxes scream to talk to each other or to find a mate. Foxes go out and about hunting for other nighttime animals such as rabbits, frogs, mice and birds, while fox cubs hunt earthworms and insects.

SKUNKS

Skunks have a reputation for spraying out a super-stinky liquid near their bottom when they are frightened. But they *usually* stomp or hiss first to give a warning. Sometimes it's possible to spot skunks in the day, but they usually emerge as the sun is setting to snack on turtle eggs, insects or fruit.

PYGMY HIPPOS

These little hippos live in swamps and rivers to keep their skin cool and wet. They leave their watery hideouts by nightfall to rumble around the tropical rainforests of west Africa looking for grass, fruits, leaves and shoots to eat – hiding from leopards who'd like to eat *them*. Pygmy hippos are usually silent, though they can squeak or grunt.

UNDER THE SEA

Deep down under the sea, there's a place that sunlight simply cannot reach, ever: the midnight zone. It's here – shrouded in total darkness where it always feels like night – many creatures put on the most incredible light displays nature has ever seen.

They can glow in the dark due to bioluminescence. This is a type of light that the creatures can create through chemical reactions in their bodies, and it creates a glow-in-the-dark effect. Creatures in the deepest depths of the ocean use this super skill to lure in prey who are attracted to the bright light, and to escape predators by shocking them with their dramatically lit-up bodies, allowing them time to swim away.

DRAGONFISH

This mighty fish has a bioluminescent body covered in a ring of bone that acts as armour, as well as spots called **photophores** beneath each eye – which it uses to send out light, a bit like a torch. One spot glows red, then the other glows blue.

PELICAN EELS

These eels can absorb light. This means they can barely be seen, even when another sea creature shines a bioluminescent light on them!

ANGLERFISH

The fearsome females have a glow-in-the-dark fishing rod, which they use to lure in prey and gobble them up!

SEA CUCUMBERS

Some species have bodies that flash with bright blue, glow-in-the-dark bands, possibly to scare off anything that might like to eat them.

In waters less deep where the sunlight does reach,
lie creatures that only come out at night . . .

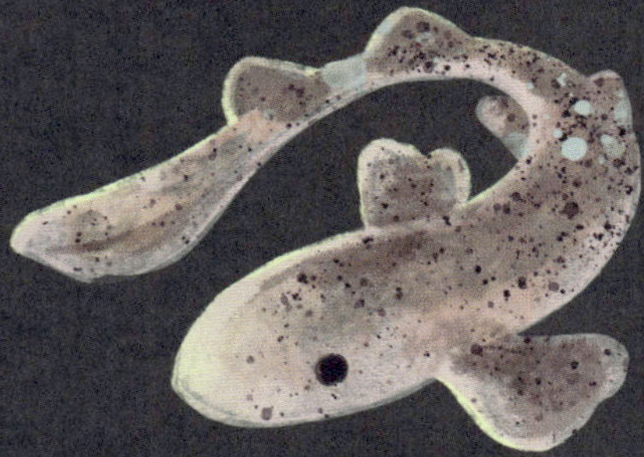

CATSHARKS

Many species sleep through the day then wake up at night to hunt crabs, molluscs and fish on the muddy sea floor.

MORAY EELS

They emerge from crevices among the coral to look for prey, ready to gobble almost any species of fish as long as they can catch it!

REPTILES

Remarkable **reptiles**, such as snakes, lizards and crocodiles, are cold-blooded animals. Some reptiles live in cool climates, whilst others live in hot places where they emerge at night to look for food when it's cooler, quieter and easier to find prey.

Amazing alligators bask in the sun during the day, then creep back into the water at night to hunt for prey. Astonishing snakes leave their leafy burrows at night to hunt for other nighttime animals, such as birds, frogs and lizards. After all, if you are a nighttime reptile, the dark is a time for hunting . . .

SALTWATER CROCODILES

Saltwater crocodiles are the biggest – and some say deadliest – reptiles in the world. They are super strong swimmers and, though these crocs live in freshwater rivers and swamps, can spend days or even weeks swimming out at sea.

These hefty crocs sleep for long periods during the day, basking in the sun, sometimes napping or hanging out underwater to cool down their bodies. But when nighttime comes, it's time for action. With glowing eyes just above the water's surface, the saltwater crocodile waits and carefully watches out for something thirsty to stop nearby and then . . . CRUNCH! It's dinnertime. Their diet consists of a long list of animals, including monkeys, wild boar, buffalo, turtles, snakes, birds – and even sharks, when they're out at sea!

The ancestors of crocodiles have been around for over 240 million years. That means they ***evolved*** *on Earth before dinosaurs!*

Crocodiles can sleep with one eye open! While they are snoozing, only one side of a crocodile's brain rests. This means that while the left side of its brain is active, the right side of its brain is resting. After a while it swaps around, and the right side is active while the left side rests. Strangely, the eye that stays open is always on the 'resting' side – so while the right side of the brain is sleeping, the right eye will stay open.

ALLIGATORS

They may look similar to crocodiles, but alligators are darker in colour with a slightly rounder (or broader) snout. Alligators can be active at all hours but prefer to hunt at night. After a lovely hot day of lying in the sun, alligators crawl into the water to search for frogs, fish, mammals and birds to eat, surfacing every 20–30 minutes to breathe. Watch out for their eyes glowing red in the dark!

RHINOCEROS VIPERS

Wait! A rhino isn't a reptile . . . this unusual-looking snake is, though. Hiding in leaf litter during the day, rhinoceros vipers are poisonous snakes that like to come out at night. Though they spend most of their time on the ground hunting rodents, these vipers are also sometimes found in trees or in water searching for frogs and fish.

GREEN TREE PYTHONS

Young green tree pythons hunt smaller creatures during the day, but the adult snakes prefer the dark where they can hunt bigger prey! These snakes have special heat sensors on their body, helping them to detect other animals, such as rodents and lizards. Once a python has sensed a meal, it wiggles its tail to attract the curious creature . . . then gobbles it up when it comes close enough.

BANDY-BANDY SNAKES

The bandy-bandy snake finds shelter during the day under rocks, in hollow logs or by digging a burrow. It then emerges at night . . . to eat other snakes! It is sometimes called the hoop snake as it can raise parts of its body off the ground in hoop-like arches. This is probably to confuse or to intimidate predators.

BLIND SNAKES

The long, pink-looking creature that's just emerged from its muddy burrow may look like a worm, but it's actually a snake! Blind snakes venture out in the dark to snack on tasty ants and termites, including their eggs and larvae. They have tiny dots for eyes and are almost entirely blind. They wiggle around very carefully as they have many predators, including hoop snakes, owls, foxes and cats.

PIT VIPERS

These snakes hide away on the leaves of large plants or in trees during the day and emerge at night to eat lizards, frogs and birds. Though it grows to just 80 centimetres long, it's highly venomous!

ALLIGATOR SNAPPING TURTLES

At night, alligator snapping turtles emerge from their cosy daytime burrows at the bottom of muddy waters to look for plants, insects, frogs and mammals to eat.

Alligator snapping turtles can stay underwater for around 45 minutes before they must come up for air.

These snappy turtles don't have teeth! But they do have very strong jaws, as well as a worm-like tongue that they use to attract prey. After all, fish like a nice juicy worm to eat! Alligator snapping turtles can't hide their heads fully into their shells like other turtles, so they 'SNAP' at predators to defend themselves instead.

GILA MONSTERS

There are very few venomous lizards in the world, but the Gila monster is one of them. They are covered in a coat of armoured bumps – tiny pieces of bone within their skin. Gila monsters spend their days hiding out underground in their desert burrows. They don't really like the heat, so they emerge at night to hunt when it's cooler. They love to eat birds and their eggs and chicks, rodents, rabbits, hares, other lizards, and bugs such as worms.

When a Gila monster bites down on its prey, ***venom*** *is released from its bottom jaw, which then travels through its teeth and into the blood of its victim. Ouch!*

Gila monsters are slow but cunning. Instead of chasing their prey, they wait for it to pass by – then attack. During the cold winter months, these reptiles stay underground to keep warm. They can store fat inside their tails, so can go for long periods without eating.

AMPHIBIANS

Amazing **amphibians** are vertebrates (animals with backbones) that need a source of water or a moist habitat to survive but can live on both land and in water. Because they often live in dark, damp places, burrowing down at the bottoms of ponds, rivers or swamps, they have adapted to survive in very dim light.

Frogs and toads have special eyes that can see in colour even when it's so dark that humans can barely see at all! However, other amphibians, such as caecilians, have poor eyesight, so they rely on other super senses to help them find food in the dark.

FROGS

Who's that croaking in the dark? It's a frog! Many species of frog come out at night to hop around looking for food. Their bulging eyes are built to see forwards, to the side, and a little bit behind them too, which helps them to spot predators. A useful trick, especially in the dark when it's more difficult to see!

Unlike humans, frogs can see in colour in the dark – helpful for clambering up trees and hopping through branches that take extra care to navigate!

RED-EYED TREE FROGS

They are thought to use their bright red eyes to shock predators so they can quickly hop away.

GRAY TREE FROGS

These amphibians spend the night looking for insects to eat. They produce a sticky fluid from the tips of their digits (the 'fingers' of a frog) so they can grip trees when they climb.

SPRING PEEPERS

When these frogs whistle at night, it means spring has arrived!

The big bubble on its throat is its vocal sac. It inflates when a spring peeper wants to make a noise. PEEP!

COMMON FROGS

In winter, they like to rest in the mud at the bottom of a pond, but in spring and summer, they spend their nights feeding on woodlice, moths and other tasty bugs.

POLKA-DOT TREE FROGS

They glow in the dark! Scientists think this is a way of communicating with other polka-dot tree frogs, possibly to find a mate.

TOADS

Toads have shorter legs than frogs and bumpy skin that looks like it's covered in warts. They don't hop around as much as frogs, and their jelly-like eggs stick together in neat long lines, unlike frogs, whose eggs come together in big clumps of jelly, called frogspawn. Like frogs, many toads are nocturnal, with incredible eyesight in the dark.

Scientists think most toads can see in colour at nighttime, just like frogs can.

AXOLOTLS

Is there anything quite as cool as an axolotl? This nocturnal species of salamander has both **gills** (the body part that helps an animal breathe underwater) *and* **lungs**, which is rare, even for an amphibian. Axolotls are critically endangered, which means there are very few left in the wild. They can be found only in one place on Earth, which is Lake Xochimilco (say SO-chee-MILL-koh) and its surrounding waters, in Mexico.

Perhaps the coolest thing about an axolotl is that they can regrow body parts – which even includes its brain, heart and lungs!

Axolotls have weak eyesight, so they sniff out their prey of molluscs, crustaceans and fish. And because they have no teeth, axolotls crush their prey by sucking it!

GIANT CAECILIANS

Legless and mostly blind, the majority of caecilians are burrowing land animals that live much of their life underground in total darkness. They listen out for vibrations which might mean prey is about to pass by and then gobble them whole. Earthworms are one of their favourite foods!

Living in Ecuador, the giant caecilian is only known to pop out of its burrow at night during a tropical storm, where it can sometimes be spotted swimming in a stream, like this one.

Aquatic caecilians live in rivers in Colombia and Venezuela. They hide in soil beds during the day and emerge after dark to munch on fish.

BUGS

Beautiful bugs of all shapes and sizes love to flutter, skitter, sing and race under the light of the stars and Moon above them. In the dark, other bugs light up caves with their beautiful glowing bottoms.

When nighttime flowers open their magnificent petals to face the Moon, insects get busy gathering pollen that bees and butterflies haven't collected during the day. Centipedes start their race to find food, and ants pick up the pace to build magnificent nests . . .

MOTHS

Meet Earth's heroes of the dark – moths. During the day, butterflies and bees are busy visiting Earth's blooms, spreading pollen to help grow new beautiful flowers. Moths do this job at night, though not all moths are nocturnal.

HAWK MOTHS

To suck up nectar from moonflowers that shine in the dark, hawk moths use their long mouthpart, called a **proboscis**.

ANGLE SHADES MOTH CATERPILLARS

Many caterpillars are nocturnal too! These ones feed on stinging nettles and prickly brambles.

In the dark, flowers such as yuccas and moonflowers glow as their pale petals reflect the moonlight, meaning moths can easily spot them. Moths visit the flowers to drink the nectar with their long, sticky mouthparts. As they do this, their small, furry bodies also pick up the pollen from the male part of the flower, called the stamen (which consists of the anther – where pollen is produced – and the filament). They then carry this to the next flower they visit, and it rubs off on the female part of the flower (the stigma) and travels to the ovary (another female part) to form seeds. This is called pollination. Without pollination, many plants would die out.

CENTIPEDES

You hardly ever see a centipede during the day, as they prefer to hide away in dark, damp places. But when they're wandering about at night, speedy centipedes can cover the length of this book in less than a second as they chase after prey such as spiders, slugs and worms! *And* they can run backwards as quickly as they can run forwards. Their front legs contain venom, which they use to kill their prey.

FUNGUS GNAT LARVAE

In the dark, the larvae (young) of the peculiar sounding fungus gnat have a secret glowing superpower . . . they spin sticky dangling webs a bit like fishing lines, light them up with their bioluminescent glow-in-the-dark bottoms and then wait for tasty prey, such as moths and mayflies, to get trapped in them.

Once something gets trapped in the larva's sticky silk, it's reeled in and gobbled up.

CRICKETS

Though many crickets sing through the day to attract a mate, most are more active during the night. It is easier to hear them at night too as it's less noisy than during the day. Like so many other living creatures, crickets use the darkness to hide from predators.

ANTS

You might think ants never have a nap. After all, have you ever *seen* one sleeping? They do sleep though – kind of. Or at least they rest, which is usually what an ant is doing when it's standing still. Some species of worker ant are said to take up to 250 one-minute naps in a 24-hour period. That adds up to over four hours!

While some ants rest around the clock, scientists think carpenter ants and sugar ants do most of their building and foraging in the darkness of night without resting much. They are very busy, so no wonder there's little time for a nap!

DARK IS SPECTACULAR

So now you know that the DARK is incredible, astonishing . . . and remarkable! By the time you wake up in the morning, SO many incredible things you can only dream about will have happened during the DARK. Take a look!

Today, more flowers will grow thanks to the amazing moths, beetles and other insects that carried the pollen from flower to flower during the night. Eggs laid while the Moon was out are now waiting to be hatched. Birds have travelled huge distances across oceans and seas under starlit skies to meet up with their feathered friends. And not only that . . .

Races have been won, songs have been sung, food has been gobbled, water has been found and poo has been hidden. And it all happened in the dark!

But for now . . .

. . . it's time for daytime animals like you to wake up and enjoy the wonderful world around us. Meanwhile, nighttime animals are tucked up in their dens, burrows, nests and other cosy spots, sleeping until it's time for their next adventure into the dark.

GLOSSARY

ALGAE A type of plant that grows near or in water with no stems or leaves. It makes much of the world's oxygen.

AMPHIBIANS Cold-blooded animals with backbones that usually lay their eggs in water and need a source of water or moist habitat to survive.

ANTENNAE A pair of long, thin body parts on an insect's head used to sense things or feel with.

COMPASS An instrument that uses Earth's magnetic field to show the direction of north.

DIURNAL Most active during the day rather than the night.

EARTH'S MAGNETIC FIELD As Earth rotates it creates a kind of magnet that can be used to locate the true direction of north.

ENDANGERED A type of animal at risk from extinction (dying out).

EVOLVED Changed gradually over many years.

GILLS Body parts or organs that animals such as fish and amphibians use to extract oxygen from water (breathe).

LEAF LITTER Plant material that has fallen to the ground.

LUNGS The body parts of organs that humans and some other animals use to breathe in oxygen from the air.

MAMMALS Animal that usually have hair, are warm-blooded and feed their young with milk.

MILKY WAY The galaxy that includes the Solar System and Earth.

NOCTURNAL Most active during the night rather than the day.

PHOTOPHORES Cells that produce light.

PIGMENTS The substances found in plants or animals that give them their colour.

PREDATORS Animals that hunt other animals as food.

PREY An animal that is hunted by another animal as food.

PROBOSCIS The long body part, shaped like a tube, attached to the head of some animals, which could be be a mouthpart or nose.

REPTILES Cold-blooded animals that lay eggs and often have scales covering their bodies.

VENOM A poisonous substance created by some animals and plants.

INDEX

ABOUT THE AUTHOR

SASKIA GWINN has spent over 20 years carefully crafting books to inspire kids. She previously worked as Head of Children's Non-fiction for Bloomsbury Publishing. Saskia has written and published award-winning books for almost every age and on nearly every topic. Saskia lives in Hertfordshire with her two boys who hope dinosaurs will one day revisit Earth.

ABOUT THE ILLUSTRATOR

CAROLINA RABEI has loved drawing since she was very small. She studied Fine Art, attaining a BA in Graphic Design in Moldova and then in Children's Book Illustration at the Cambridge School of Art. Carolina's stunning first picture book illustrating Walter de la Mare's poem, 'Snow', was published to much critical acclaim and nominated for the esteemed Kate Greenaway Medal.